QUARRY MONSTERS

For Kids

These massive machines build our world!

Lucy James

Copyright © 2022 Arrowtown Press

Published by Arrowtown Press

Huntly
New Zealand 3700

info@arrowtownpress.com

All rights reserved. Reproduction in whole or in part without written permission of the publisher is strictly prohibited.

Check out more children's books at Lucy's Amazon page:
https://tinyurl.com/5n7huh46.

Table of Contents

Introduction	1
Chapter 1: The Marvels of Quarries	4
Chapter 2: The Mighty Bagger 288	10
Chapter 3: The Colossal BelAZ 75710	15
Chapter 4: The Amazing Marion 6360	19
Chapter 5: The Monster Hitachi EH5000AC-3	23
Chapter 6: The Mighty Komatsu D575A-3 Super Dozer	28
The Final Word	32

Introduction

Welcome, young adventurers, to the world of gigantic quarry machines! Get ready to embark on an extraordinary journey where we'll explore the colossal machines that shape our landscapes and unearth treasures hidden beneath the Earth's surface.

Imagine standing before a towering monster, a machine so massive it makes tall buildings look like tiny toys. These colossal machines are the giants of quarrying and mining. They move mountains and transform the landscape around us. From the thunderous roar of engines to the ground-shaking rumble of tires, these mighty machines command attention wherever they go. They are more than just machines; they are titans that shape our world.

Quarry machines are amazing - and so are the people who operate them!

Picture massive trucks that can carry loads heavier than a hundred elephants. Envision bulldozers with blades so huge they can level hills in a single sweep. Visualize excavators with arms that reach to the sky, scooping up enormous quantities of earth and rocks. These machines are the superheroes of the quarrying world wielding immense power and strength.

These are Sinomach machines. Sinomach is a Chinese company.

But how are these colossal machines built? How do they work? And what makes them so special? Together, we'll dive into their incredible features, learn about their mind-boggling dimensions, and discover the science behind their remarkable capabilities.

We'll meet the Bagger 288, a mammoth excavator that could swallow cars in a single scoop. We'll marvel at the BelAZ 75710, a hauling truck that can carry the weight of hundreds of elephants. We'll witness the Marion 6360, a colossal walking dragline that reaches higher than skyscrapers. And we'll uncover the secrets of the Komatsu D575A-3, a super dozer that can move mountains with its amazing power.

So, fasten your seatbelts and prepare for an exhilarating look at gigantic quarry machines. Get ready to be amazed, inspired, and filled with awe as we uncover the engineering marvels that shape our world. Are you ready? Let's set off on this incredible adventure together!

Chapter 1: The Marvels of Quarries

Before we dive into the magnificent machines found in quarries, we should have a quick look at why we need quarries and the important role they play in our modern world.

This is the Mir diamond mine in Siberia, Russia.

Another view of the Mir diamond mine.

Have you ever wondered where the rocks, stones, and minerals that we use to build our wonderful world come from? Well, many of them are found deep within the Earth's crust, hiding in a special place called a quarry. In this chapter, we'll explore the nature of quarries, why they are important, and why we need huge machines to work them.

What is a Quarry? A quarry is a place where large-scale excavation takes place to extract valuable resources from the ground. It's like a treasure trove of rocks and minerals waiting to be discovered. Quarries can be found all around the world and come in different sizes and shapes, depending on what is being extracted.

Heavy rock breakers in action at Birla Cements' limestone mines, India.

The Importance of Quarries: Quarries play a vital role in our lives. They provide us with the materials needed to build our homes, schools, and even playgrounds. Stones and rocks from quarries are used to construct roads, bridges, and buildings. Minerals extracted from quarries are used in everything from electronics to jewelry. Quarries are the starting point for many industries, making them essential for our modern way of life.

This is the Birros marble quarry in Greece.

Birros marble quarry.

Digging Deep: Quarries are all about digging deep into the Earth to uncover valuable resources. To do this, powerful machines are needed. Excavators, such as the Bagger 288, use giant buckets to scoop up massive amounts of rocks and minerals from the ground. These machines are equipped with advanced technology that allows them to dig deep and efficiently, making the excavation process faster and safer.

Hauling the Load: Once the rocks and minerals are excavated, they need to be transported to their destination. This is where colossal hauling trucks, like the BelAZ 75710, come into play. These trucks can carry enormous loads, moving the materials from the quarry to processing plants or construction sites. With their immense size and powerful engines, these hauling trucks make the transportation process efficient and effective.

Two huge quarry trucks haul gold ore from a mine in Australia.

Safety First: Working in a quarry requires careful attention to safety. Quarry workers use advanced technology to protect themselves and ensure a safe working environment. From specialized safety clothing to monitoring systems that detect potential hazards, technology plays a crucial role in safeguarding workers and preventing accidents.

A Bagger 288 roadblock!

Environmental Responsibility: Quarry operators are mindful of their impact on the environment. They use technology to minimize disturbances to surrounding ecosystems. Techniques such as reclamation and restoration are employed to restore quarried areas back to their natural state once the resources have been extracted. This ensures that the land can be reused for other purposes, like agriculture or conservation, after the quarrying process is complete.

Quarries are fascinating places where nature and technology intertwine. They provide us with the materials we need for construction and manufacturing while also ensuring responsible land use. The technology used in quarries allows us to extract resources efficiently, transport them safely, and protect the environment.

Next time you see a building, a road, or a sparkling piece of jewelry, remember that it all starts with quarries and the incredible technology behind them. Quarries are the hidden heroes that help shape our world.

Chapter 2: The Mighty Bagger 288

Built by: ThyssenKrupp, Germany

Entered Service: 1978

Length: 721 ft

Width: 251 ft

Height: 315 ft

Weight: 29,800,000 lb

In the world of enormous machines, there is one that stands taller and mightier than the rest. Its name is Bagger 288, and it holds the title of the largest excavator in the world.

The Bagger 288 is so monstrous that it features in video games.

10

A Gigantic Giant: The Bagger 288 is a true giant among giants. Standing at a towering height of 220 feet, it is taller than a seven-story building. Its length stretches over 700 feet, which is more than two football fields put together. This mighty machine weighs a staggering 13,500 tons, equivalent to around 8,600 cars!

A Powerful Digging Force: The primary purpose of the Bagger 288 is to excavate, or dig up, enormous amounts of material. It is mainly used in mining operations, including quarrying, to extract coal, minerals, and other valuable resources from the Earth. This colossal excavator can dig up to 240,000 tons of material every day, which is equal to the weight of around 8 0,000 elephants! Its digging capability is truly mind-boggling.

The Bagger 288 literally tears up the land with its wheel.

An Enormous Bucket Wheel: At the heart of the Bagger 288 lies its gigantic bucket wheel. This wheel is covered in a series of large buckets, similar to those on a waterwheel. As the wheel turns, the buckets scoop up the material from the ground and dump it on a conveyor belt system. The wheel alone has a diameter of over 70 feet, making it one of the largest in the world. The power of the Bagger's bucket wheel is simply astonishing!

The Bagger 288 dominates the landscape.

A Team Effort: Operating the Bagger 288 requires a skilled team of operators and engineers. The machine needs a crew of several people to control its movements, manage its functions, and ensure everything runs smoothly. Each member of the team plays a vital role in making the Bagger 288 work efficiently and safely. It takes great coordination and expertise to handle such a massive machine.

Transporting the Bagger 288: You might be wondering how this colossal machine reaches its work sites. Well, the Bagger 288 is not easily moved from one place to another. It was actually assembled right at its original location in Germany. The parts were brought in by trucks, ships, and trains, and then carefully assembled to form the massive machine we see today. Once assembled, the Bagger 288 stays at the site until its job is done.

At night the Bagger 288 is even more imposing. Can you see the little car under the Bagger's wheel?

The Bagger 288 is a true engineering marvel. Its enormous size and incredible digging power make it an extraordinary machine in the world of mining and quarrying.

Next time you imagine yourself operating a powerful excavator, think about the mighty Bagger 288 and the tremendous tasks it can accomplish. With its remarkable capabilities, it truly deserves its place in the record books as the king of excavators!

The business end of the Bagger 288.

Chapter 3: The Colossal BelAZ 75710

Built by: BelAZ, Belorussia

Entered Service: 2013

Length: 67 ft 7 in

Width: 32 ft 4 in

Height: 27 ft 1 in

Weight: 793664 lb

In the realm of enormous trucks, there is one that reigns supreme as the largest of them all – the BelAZ 75710!

A brand new BelAZ 75710.

15

A Giant of the Roads: The BelAZ 75710 is no ordinary truck - it's a true giant on wheels! With a length of over 67 feet and a height of almost 33 feet, this massive truck is taller than a three-story building and longer than two school buses lined up together. Its sheer size is awe-inspiring and makes it a behemoth on the roads.

A Payload Powerhouse: One of the most impressive features of the BelAZ 75710 is its exceptional payload capacity. This colossal truck can carry an astounding 450 tons of material, equivalent to the weight of about 375 small cars or 225 elephants! It's like having a small mountain of materials on the move. The BelAZ 75710 is a true powerhouse when it comes to carrying heavy loads.

Engines That Roar: To propel this enormous truck forward, it requires an incredibly powerful engine. The BelAZ 75710 is equipped with a colossal engine that generates 11,000 horsepower. That's equivalent to around 450 small cars combined! This mighty engine ensures that the truck has enough power to conquer the steepest inclines and roughest terrains.

Tire Tales: The wheels of the BelAZ 75710 are no ordinary wheels—they are colossal in size. Each tire stands over 13 feet tall, which is taller than most houses! To withstand the massive weight it carries, each tire is specially designed with multiple layers of strong and durable materials. These giant tires help the truck roll smoothly along the roads, providing stability and reliability.

Complex Assembly: Building the BelAZ 75710 is a remarkable feat in itself. Its various parts are manufactured in different locations and then transported to a special assembly facility. Skilled engineers and workers carefully piece together all the components, ensuring they fit perfectly to create this mammoth truck. The process requires precision, teamwork, and expertise to construct this colossal vehicle.

A Champion of Efficiency: While the BelAZ 75710 is a mighty giant, it is also mindful of efficiency. Its advanced technology helps optimize fuel consumption and reduces emissions, making it more environmentally friendly than older trucks. Despite its colossal size, the BelAZ 75710 aims to balance power and efficiency, demonstrating that even massive machines can be conscious of the environment.

The BelAZ 75710 is a true titan on the roads. Its colossal size, jaw-dropping payload capacity, and powerful engine make it an awe-inspiring marvel. The next time you see a truck, imagine the extraordinary capabilities of the BelAZ 75710 and wonder at the incredible engineering that goes into creating such a colossal machine.

A big truck needs a big garage. Can you see the people standing on the truck's front deck?

A big load for the big BelAZ 75710.

18

Chapter 4: The Amazing Marion 6360

Built by: Marion Power Shovel, Ohio, USA

Entered Service: 1965

Length: 319 ft

Width: 88 ft

Height: 210 ft

Weight: 28,000,000 lb

In the realm of enormous machines, there is one that stands out as a true titan—the Marion 6360, also known as "The Captain." The Captain is one of the largest walking draglines ever built. A dragline is a quarry machine that has a large bucket suspended from a boom by a system of wire cables. The bucket is lifted, lowered and turned with these cables.

Meet "The Captain": The Captain, as it is fondly called by the workers who operate the dragline, stands at a towering height of 310 feet. It reaches higher than a 30-story building! Its colossal size and power make it a legendary figure in the world of mining and quarrying.

The Mighty Marion 6360.

Gigantic Weight: The Captain is not just tall but also incredibly heavy. With a weight of around 13,000 tons, it weighs as much as about 1,300 elephants combined! To put it in perspective, it's like having more than 4,000 cars stacked together. Its immense weight enables it to stay balanced and stable while it performs its mining operations.

Digging into the Earth: The primary purpose of the Captain is to dig up vast amounts of earth and rock. It works seven days a week and fills 150 railroad carloads of coal a day. Equipped with an enormous bucket, it can scoop up to 160 cubic yards of material in a single scoop. That's equivalent to filling up around 80 standard bathtubs! With each swing of its mighty arm, it removes massive quantities of material from the ground.

The Marion 6360 working at the coal face.

It Walks on Giant Legs: The Captain has both tracks and legs. Each leg is over 90 feet long and weighs as much as several small cars. By lifting and swinging its legs, the Captain can slowly move across the mining site to reach different areas of excavation. Its walking ability gives it the flexibility to tackle large areas efficiently.

The mechanism on the right side of this dragline is a leg and shoe. Each leg swings forward and then the shoe takes the weight as the machine moves to its next location in the quarry.

Powerful Electric Heart: Inside the Captain's colossal frame resides a mighty heart - a massive electric motor system. Four generator sets convert 14,000 volts of AC power into DC power for the twenty main-drive motors. This complex electric system produces about 30,000 horsepower. This energy powers the arm's movements, leg walking motion, and all other vital functions of the Captain.

A Crew of Experts: Operating the Captain is no small feat. It requires a highly skilled team of operators and engineers. The operators control the machine's movements and functions, while the engineers ensure its mechanical and electrical systems are in top shape. It takes a dedicated and knowledgeable crew to tame this mighty beast and make it work with precision.

The Marion 6360 is an awe-inspiring giant among machines. Its towering height, immense weight, and powerful digging capabilities make it an extraordinary force in the world of mining and quarrying.

Chapter 5: The Monster Hitachi EH5000AC-3

Built by: Hitachi Construction Machinery, Japan

Entered Service: 2013

Length: 51 ft

Width: 31.5 ft

Height: 32 ft

Weight: 38,360,433 pounds

In the world of colossal machines, there is one that stands tall and mighty - the Hitachi EH5000AC-3.

The Hitachi in its natural environment.

A Titan of Hauling: The Hitachi EH5000AC-3 is no ordinary truck - it is a true titan of hauling. With a payload capacity of up to 320 tons, it can carry an astonishing amount of material. Picture a load as heavy as 160 elephants or nearly 300 cars! This colossal truck is built to transport large quantities of rocks, minerals, or other valuable resources from one place to another with exceptional power and efficiency.

Enormous Size: When it comes to size, the Hitachi EH5000AC-3 doesn't disappoint. It stretches over 50 feet in length, which is longer than a large shipping container. It also stands at a height of over 30 feet, towering over most buildings. The sheer dimensions of this truck make it an impressive sight to behold.

It takes a convoy to transport the Hitachi EH5000ACV-3.

Power on Wheels: To propel this colossal machine, the Hitachi EH5000AC-3 relies on a mighty engine. It boasts an incredible power output of over 2,700 horsepower, which is equivalent to the combined power of around 180 small cars! This immense power allows the truck to conquer steep inclines and challenging terrains effortlessly.

Rugged Tires: The Hitachi EH5000AC-3's tires are not your ordinary wheels - they are rugged and built for the toughest conditions. Each tire measures over 13 feet in diameter. These massive tires are specially designed to withstand heavy loads and rough terrains, providing stability and durability as the truck makes its way through the mining or quarrying site.

The Hitachi EH5000AC-3 is a powerful and compact-looking machine.

Advanced Technology: The Hitachi EH5000AC-3 incorporates advanced technology to optimize its performance. It features an intelligent computer system that monitors various aspects of the truck's operation, such as engine performance, fuel consumption, and maintenance needs. This smart technology helps ensure the truck operates efficiently and effectively, reducing downtime and maximizing productivity.

The Team behind the Machine: Operating and maintaining the Hitachi EH5000AC-3 requires a skilled and dedicated team of professionals. From the drivers who maneuver this colossal truck to the technicians who conduct regular inspections and repairs, every member plays a crucial role. Their expertise and teamwork keep the machine running smoothly, ensuring safe and efficient operations.

The Hitachi EH5000AC-3 is a true giant in the world of quarry trucks. Its massive size, remarkable payload capacity, and powerful performance make it an awe-inspiring machine. The next time you see a truck on the road, imagine the incredible capabilities of the Hitachi EH5000AC-3 and perhaps think about the engineering skills that make such colossal machines possible.

The Hitachi dumps a load.

27

Chapter 6: The Mighty Komatsu D575A-3 Super Dozer

Built by: Komatsu Ltd.

Entered Service: 1991

Length: 38 feet 5 inches

Width: 24 feet 3 inches

Height: 16 feet

Weight: 336,400 lb

The Komatsu has an enormous front blade.

In the world of bulldozers, there is one that reigns supreme—the Komatsu D575A-3 Super Dozer.

Meet the Super Dozer: The Komatsu D575A-3 Super Dozer is not your ordinary bulldozer - it is a true titan among its kind. With a length of over 39 feet and a height of almost 17 feet, it towers over most buildings. Its sheer size is awe-inspiring and makes it a formidable force in the world of mines and quarries.

Earth-Shifting Power: The primary purpose of the Super Dozer is to move massive amounts of earth and rocks. Equipped with a mighty blade, it can push and level large quantities of material with ease. The blade capacity of the Komatsu D575A-3 is over 90 cubic yards. That is the same as an average swimming pool of dirt moved with each swipe!

The Komatsu has more than 1000 horsepower to push stone, dirt and gravel around the quarry.

Unmatched Strength: To generate the tremendous force needed for its tasks, the Super Dozer relies on its powerful diesel engine. The Komatsu D575A-3 boasts an astonishing engine output of over 1,150 horsepower. That's equivalent to the combined power of about 70 small cars! This immense strength enables the Super Dozer to tackle even the toughest terrains and push through obstacles effortlessly.

Tracks for Stability: Unlike traditional wheeled vehicles, the Super Dozer moves on tracks, just like a tank. These massive tracks provide stability and distribute the machine's weight evenly, ensuring it remains steady even on uneven or challenging surfaces.

Building with Precision: While the Super Dozer is known for its strength, it also possesses remarkable precision. It is equipped with advanced technology that allows the operator to control the blade with accuracy. This precision ensures that the Super Dozer can perform delicate tasks, such as creating precise slopes or levelling surfaces, with utmost control and efficiency.

The Operator's Expertise: Behind the controls of the Super Dozer is a skilled operator. The operator's expertise is vital in maneuvering this colossal machine and utilizing its power effectively. With their knowledge and experience, they can navigate rough tracks, operate the blade with precision, and ensure safety while maximizing the Super Dozer's capabilities.

The Komatsu D575A-3 Super Dozer is a true titan among construction machines. Its colossal size, earth-moving power, and precision make it an awe-inspiring marvel.

The Final Word

Hi there,

I hope you enjoyed reading about the huge earth movers that shape the world around us. I live in a town in New Zealand that has produced coal for well over 100 years. There are plenty of quarries within a short walk of my place. The next three photos show some of these quarries. The last photo shows Lake Puketirini which is a former coal pit that has been developed into a lake. Lake Puketirini is 64 metres deep at its deepest point and is now used for many activities such as swimming, kayaking and scuba dive training.

Thanks again for taking a look at my book! All the best...

Lucy

Huntly quarry.

Huntly coal mine.

Lake Puketirini, a former Huntly coal mine pit.

More of Lucy's books that might interest you. You can find them all on Amazon at https://tinyurl.com/5n7huh46.

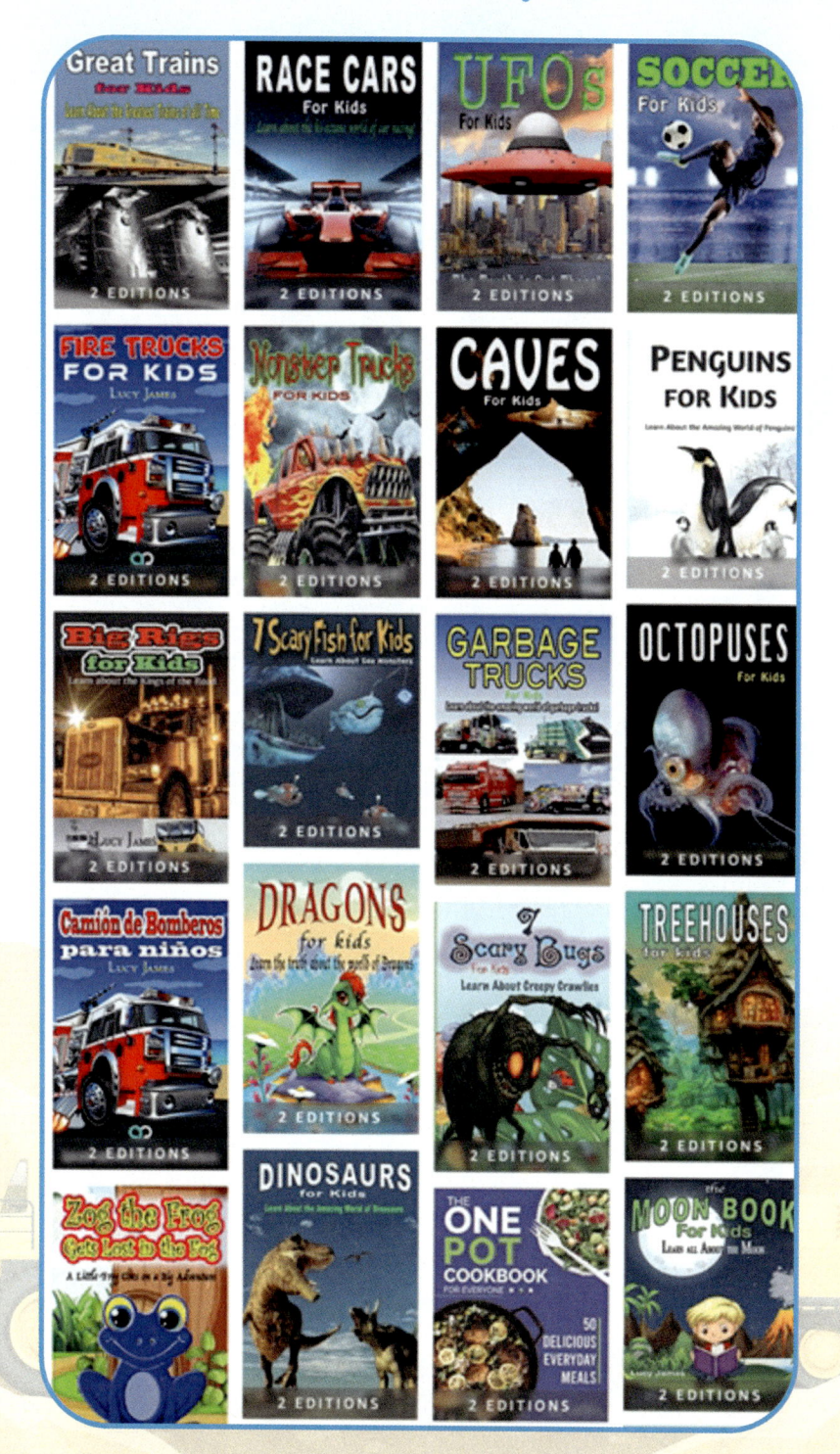